It's Moving Day!

Written by Pamela Hickman

Illustrated by Geraldo Valério

Kids Can Press

To my three daughters,
who are growing up and moving out — PH

To Orminda — GV

Text © 2008 Pamela Hickman
Illustrations © 2008 Geraldo Valério

Kids Can Press acknowledges the financial support of the Government of Ontario, through the Ontario Media Development Corporation's Ontario Book Initiative; the Ontario Arts Council; the Canada Council for the Arts; and the Government of Canada, through the BPIDP, for our publishing activity.

Published in Canada by
Kids Can Press Ltd.
29 Birch Avenue
Toronto, ON M4V 1E2

Published in the U.S. by
Kids Can Press Ltd.
2250 Military Road
Tonawanda, NY 14150

www.kidscanpress.com

The artwork in this book was rendered in acrylic.
The text is set in Catseye.

Edited by Stacey Roderick and Yvette Ghione
Designed by Marie Bartholomew
Printed and bound in Canada

This book is smyth sewn casebound.

CM 08 0 9 8 7 6 5 4 3 2

Library and Archives Canada Cataloguing in Publication

Hickman, Pamela
    It's moving day / written by Pamela Hickman ; illustrated by Geraldo Valério.

ISBN 978-1-55453-074-8

1. Burrowing animals—Juvenile literature. 2. Soil animals—Juvenile literature. 3. Animals—Habitations—Juvenile literature. I. Valerio, Geraldo II. Title.

QL756.15.H53 2008   591.56'48   C2007-902957-4

Kids Can Press is a ʃOrʊs™ Entertainment company

The burrow lies hidden beneath
a big tree on the edge of a field.

After a long winter's sleep, the woodchuck climbs out of his underground home and stretches.

Time to dig his summer home down in the farmer's pasture where there is more food to eat.

It's moving day!

A nervous cottontail rabbit hops over to the empty burrow and sniffs around. It is the perfect place to raise her family.

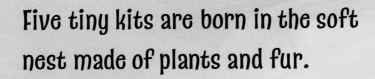

Five tiny kits are born in the soft
nest made of plants and fur.

The kits grow quickly. Soon they
leave home to be on their own.

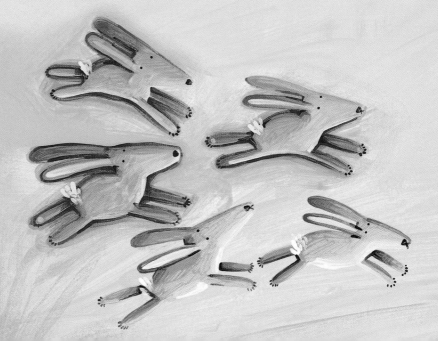

The mother cottontail raises another family and, by fall, all of her young have moved away.

Winter is coming, and the cottontail must hurry. She leaves the burrow to find a winter home.

It's moving day!

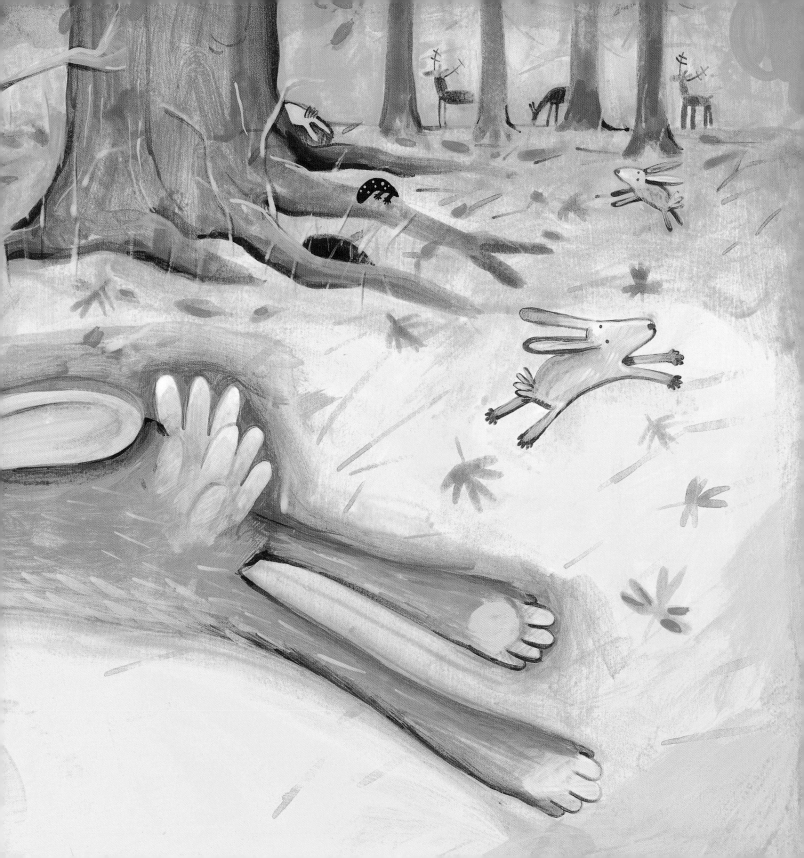

The late fall air is cold, and the yellow-spotted salamander can't move very quickly.

He reaches the burrow just in time
and crawls inside, safe for the winter.

Spring rain and warm winds wake the salamander from his winter sleep.

He heads to the nearest woodland pool to meet other salamanders. In a few days, hundreds of salamander eggs will be laid there.

It's moving day!

Her tree house destroyed by the spring storm, the raccoon searches for a new home where her kits can be born. She's in luck!

The baby raccoons grow quickly over the summer.
In the fall, the raccoon and her family eat so much
that they get big and fat. Now they are ready for a
long winter underground.

The family spends most of the winter cuddled
up together in the burrow, sleeping.

The young raccoons leave their mother in the spring to make room for her next family.

One late summer morning, she smells a fox nearby and knows it isn't safe. She carries her new babies to another home, away from danger.

It's moving day!

The empty burrow is just what the milk snake
is looking for. As the days grow cooler, more
snakes gather to share the winter shelter.

Under the snowy ground, the snakes sleep in a heap for the winter.

The sleeping snakes are woken by the warm spring sun.
They slither away from the burrow to search for food.

It's moving day!

Now that the snakes have left and it is safe, a chipmunk scurries over to inspect the empty burrow.

The chipmunk wastes no time moving in. She makes a comfortable nest of leaves and dried grasses before her six pups are born.

By the end of summer, the young chipmunks are fully grown. It's time to leave their mother and find their own homes.

In the fall, while she is nibbling on some seeds, the chipmunk senses an enemy approaching. She scurries into the woods and leaves the burrow behind.

It's moving day!

A passing skunk is pleased with her find. She squeezes in and settles down to sleep through the cold winter.

The skunk and her five new babies
snuggle inside their cozy home while
the spring weather warms up outside.

All summer long, the skunk family sleeps and plays during the day. In the evenings, they look for food. On one outing, they discover a bigger home.

It's moving day!

A plump woodchuck spots the
empty burrow while searching for
a place to dig his new winter shelter.
After cleaning it out, he is ready to climb in.

The woodchuck sleeps for six long months
until it's moving day again.

Woodchuck

Woodchucks, also called groundhogs, are related to squirrels and feed on plants. In the fall, woodchucks eat a lot to put on extra fat. Then they curl up in their burrows and sleep through winter. When they wake up in the spring, they are thin and hungry!

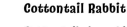

Cottontail Rabbit

Cottontails have big ears and twitchy noses that can hear and smell danger all around. The mother rabbit gives birth in spring and summer. A newborn kit would fit in your hand; it is hairless and cannot see. Within a couple of weeks, the kits can hop around and feed on plants. Cottontails stay active all year long.

Yellow-spotted Salamander

Yellow-spotted salamanders are related to frogs and toads. They live on land but lay their eggs in water. Like tadpoles, salamander babies live in the water until they develop into adults. These salamanders eat insects, earthworms, slugs and snails. A yellow-spotted salamander can live for twenty years!

Raccoon

Baby raccoons are born in early spring. They cannot see or hear until they are about three weeks old. After two months, the young follow their mother out at night to find food. Raccoons eat almost anything, including insects, fruit, fish and frogs. Raccoon families may stay together for a year.

Red Fox

Foxes are related to wolves and dogs. They are shy animals but very good hunters. Their excellent hearing and sense of smell help them find small animals and birds to eat. They also feed on berries, acorns and apples. Red foxes are active all year long. They spend fall and winter alone but stay with their families the rest of the year.

Eastern Milk Snake

Snakes are reptiles, like lizards and turtles. Eastern milk snakes can grow to about a meter (3 1/4 ft.) long. They gather together in large numbers in the fall to shelter from the cold. Snakes only wake up when the air gets warmer in the spring. Female milk snakes lay up to 17 eggs in early summer.

Eastern Chipmunk

Chipmunks are part of the squirrel family. They spend most of their days gathering and storing seeds and berries to eat later. They carry the food in their huge cheek pouches. Chipmunks are good tree climbers and often sit up high and chatter at enemies or intruders.

Striped Skunk

Skunk babies are born in early spring. They are so tiny that several would fit on this page! Mother skunks use their smelly spray to protect their young from danger. The babies start spraying once they are six or seven weeks old. By late fall, the young skunks are ready to find their own burrows for the winter.